CAMBRIDGE

A2
KEY 1

WITHOUT ANSWERS

AUTHENTIC PRACTICE TESTS

T0349678

Cambridge University Press
www.cambridge.org/elt

Cambridge Assessment English
www.cambridgeenglish.org

Information on this title: www.cambridge.org/9781108718127

© Cambridge University Press and UCLES 2019

It is normally necessary for written permission for copying to be obtained
in advance from a publisher. The sample answer sheets at the back of this
book are designed to be copied and distributed in class.
The normal requirements are waived here and it is not necessary to write to
Cambridge University Press for permission for an individual teacher to make copies
for use within his or her own classroom. Only those pages that carry the wording
'© UCLES 2019 Photocopiable' may be copied.

First published 2019
20 19 18 17 16 15 14 13 12 11 10 9 8 7 6 5 4 3

Printed in Italy by Rotolito S.p.A.

A catalogue record for this publication is available from the British Library

ISBN 978-1-108-69463-6 Key 1 Student's Book with answers with Audio
ISBN 978-1-108-71812-7 Key 1 Student's Book without answers
ISBN 978-1-108-71813-4 Audio CDs (2)

The publishers have no responsibility for the persistence or accuracy of URLs
for external or third-party internet websites referred to in this publication, and
do not guarantee that any content on such websites is, or will remain, accurate
or appropriate. Information regarding prices, travel timetables, and other factual
information given in this work is correct at the time of first printing but the
publishers do not guarantee the accuracy of such information thereafter.

Contents

Introduction

This collection of four complete practice tests contains papers from the *Cambridge English Qualifications A2 Key* examination. Students can practise these tests on their own or with the help of a teacher.

The *A2 Key* examination is part of a series of Cambridge English Qualifications for general and higher education. This series consists of five qualifications that have similar characteristics but are designed for different levels of English language ability. The *A2 Key* certificate is recognised around the world as a basic qualification in English.

Cambridge English Qualifications	CEFR Level	UK National Qualifications Framework Level
C2 Proficiency	C2	3
C1 Advanced	C1	2
B2 First	B2	1
B1 Preliminary	B1	Entry 3
A2 Key	A2	Entry 2

Further information

The information contained in this practice book is designed to be an overview of the exam. For a full description of all of the above exams, including information about task types, testing focus and preparation, please see the relevant handbooks which can be obtained from the Cambridge Assessment English website at: **cambridgeenglish.org**.

The structure of *A2 Key*: an overview

The *Cambridge English Qualifications A2 Key* examination consists of three papers:

Reading and Writing: 60 minutes
Candidates need to be able to understand simple written information such as signs and newspapers, and produce simple written English.

Listening: 30 minutes approximately
Candidates need to show they can follow and understand a range of spoken materials such as announcements, when people speak reasonably slowly.

Speaking: 8–10 minutes
Candidates take the Speaking test with another candidate or in a group of three. They are tested on their ability to take part in different types of interaction: with the examiner, with the other candidate and by themselves.

	Overall length	Number of tasks/ parts	Number of items
Reading and Writing	60 mins	7	32
Listening	approx. 30 mins	5	25
Speaking	8–10 mins	2	–
Total	approx. 1 hour 40 mins		

Grading

All candidates receive a Statement of Results and candidates whose performance ranges between CEFR Levels A1 and B1 (Cambridge English Scale scores of 100–150) also receive a certificate.

- Candidates who achieve **Grade A** (Cambridge English Scale scores of 140–150) receive the Key English Test certificate stating that they demonstrated ability at Level B1.
- Candidates who achieve **Grade B** or **C** (Cambridge English Scale scores of 120–139) receive the Key English Test certificate at Level A2.
- Candidates whose performance is below A2 level, but falls within **Level A1** (Cambridge English Scale scores of 100–119), receive a Cambridge English certificate stating that they have demonstrated ability at Level A1.

For further information on grading and results, go to the website (see page 5 for details).

Speaking: an overview for candidates

The Speaking test lasts 8–10 minutes. You will take the test with another candidate. There are two examiners but only one of them will talk to you. The examiner will ask you questions and ask you to talk to the other candidate.

Part 1 (3–4 minutes)
The examiner will ask you and your partner some questions. These questions will be about your daily life, interests, likes and dislikes. For example, you may have to speak about school, hobbies or home town.

Part 2 (5–6 minutes)
You and your partner will speak to each other. The examiner will give you a card with some illustrations on it. You will then discuss the activities, things or places illustrated on the card with your partner. The examiner will then ask you and your partner some individual questions about the illustrations on the card.

Test 1

READING AND WRITING (60 minutes)

PART 1

QUESTIONS 1–6

For each question, choose the correct answer.

1

Susie,
Can you take your
work stuff out of the
living room and put
it in your room? Liz is
coming for coffee.
Chloe

Chloe wants Susie

A   to clean her room.

B   to stop working at home.

C   to tidy up the living room.

2

STUDENTS!
Cleaners are here
every Friday, but please
wash up and put things
away after you've used
the kitchen.
Thank you!

What is this message asking students to do?

A   help keep the kitchen tidy at all times

B   let the cleaners know when the kitchen's free

C   stay out of the kitchen when the cleaners are there

3

Hi Pete,
Could you get me
from the train station
later tonight? I don't
think there'll be any
taxis there. Text me
back now!
Anna

What does Anna want Pete to do?

A   order a taxi to pick her up from the station

B   text her when he gets to the station

C   give her a lift from the station

4

NEW STUDENTS

Go to Reception to collect your course books before seeing your teacher

A   New students should go to Reception before they collect their books.

B   Course books will be available at Reception for students.

C   Teachers will meet the new students at Reception.

5

Apartment for rent, Redbridge

One double bedroom

Just been painted, with new kitchen

ryt@ukmail.com

A   This flat is in a new building.

B   This flat is ready to move into.

C   This flat is too small for two people.

6

Simon,
Don't forget to bring that book I lent you to school tomorrow. It was so good I want to read it again.
Gemma

Why did Gemma contact Simon?

A   to tell him about a book she liked

B   to ask him to return her book

C   to offer to lend him a book

PART 2

QUESTIONS 7–13

For each question, choose the correct answer.

		Sandy Bay	High Wood	Black Lake
7	Which campsite has an indoor swimming pool?	A	B	C
8	Which campsite offers water sports classes?	A	B	C
9	Which campsite has great views?	A	B	C
10	Which campsite has a shop where people can buy food?	A	B	C
11	Which campsite offers evening activities?	A	B	C
12	Which campsite has lots of space for your tent?	A	B	C
13	Which campsite has bikes you can borrow?	A	B	C

Three great campsites to try this summer

Sandy Bay

This campsite is on an excellent beach, and has its own surfing school with special prices for campers. You can also learn to windsurf and sail there. The sea is safe for swimming, so it's a great place for families. The large swimming pool is great in summer, and has a wide area of grass around it. Its small supermarket has long opening hours. It doesn't matter what size tent you bring, as the campsite is large and you won't be too near your neighbours!

High Wood

There are lots of activities you can do at High Wood campsite, from fishing to cycling, and they'll lend you any of the equipment you need. It's not as large as some campsites, but it's clean and modern. It has a fantastic pool with a roof window which can open and close. There's also a special area where you can watch films or dance under the stars to local bands. For food shopping, try the shop in the nearby village.

Black Lake

The wonderful thing about Black Lake campsite is waking up in the morning and seeing the beautiful mountains all around you. You don't have to bring your own tent – there are some already there you can pay to use. There's lots to do – you can swim in the lake or walk in the forest. And don't forget to bring your mountain bike with you! If you want to cook for yourself, the shop in the next village has a good variety of food.

PART 3

QUESTIONS 14–18

For each question, choose the correct answer.

Jack Calder

Violin player Jack Calder plays in the Australian band, Ocean Blue.

Jack Calder started playing the violin when he was ten. 'My music teacher played and one day he asked if anyone wanted to learn. Some girls put up their hands and so did I. I didn't have a violin, but my uncle said I could use his. The lessons were really hard at first, but playing the violin soon became important to me.'

After leaving school, Jack moved to Melbourne. For a time, he preferred listening to music to playing it. The rock music he listened to sounded very different from violin music, so he bought an electric violin, and started putting the things he liked about rock music into the music he played on his violin.

A year later, Jack met a small group of Melbourne musicians. 'We all thought about music in the same way and started Ocean Blue together. A year later, we were playing lots of concerts, and our music was selling well. But we didn't want this to make us different people. We didn't want to stop being friends.'

Jack meets many people who think playing the violin is an unusual career, but he doesn't agree with them. 'I think it's the best thing in the world. I guess I'm lucky that way. The internet has changed music, but when I walk into a violin shop it's like entering another world – one where time has stopped. Someone has looked after these beautiful old instruments that are two or three hundred years old. I think that's amazing.'

---

14   What do we learn about Jack in the first paragraph?

    A   He was the only person at school to play the violin.

    B   He learned to play on an instrument that he borrowed.

    C   He enjoyed playing the violin as soon as he started learning.

15   What is the writer doing in the second paragraph?

    A   explaining why Jack thought some music was easy to play

    B   saying why only a few people liked the music Jack played

    C   describing how Jack changed the kind of music he played

16   What does Jack say about Ocean Blue?

    A   Nobody in the band liked travelling far to play in a concert.

    B   The band members were interested in different kinds of music.

    C   Everyone wanted to stay friends when the band became successful.

17   Why does Jack think he is lucky?

    A   He meets lots of people.

    B   He loves what he does.

    C   He has an unusual career.

18   Jack thinks it is a good idea

    A   to keep some things that people used in the past.

    B   to make more music available on the internet.

    C   to teach more people to play an instrument.

PART 4

QUESTIONS 19–24

For each question, choose the correct answer.

The London Marathon

In 1979, two British men called John Disley and Chris Brasher **(19)** .... to run the New York Marathon. This 42-kilometre race goes through the city, past many of its famous tourist sights. Disley and Brasher found that it was very different from marathons in the UK.

At that **(20)** .... in the UK, nobody was interested in marathons, but in New York, there were large **(21)** .... of people watching. Afterwards, the two men had the **(22)** .... of starting a similar race in London.

The first London Marathon was in 1981, and over six thousand runners **(23)** .... part. Since then, the race has happened every year, and has become popular with runners from all over the world. Over a million people have completed it, and it is **(24)** .... on TV in nearly 200 countries.

19	**A**	thought	**B**	said	**C**	decided

20	**A**	year	**B**	day	**C**	time

21	**A**	members	**B**	crowds	**C**	visitors

22	**A**	idea	**B**	answer	**C**	fact

23	**A**	stayed	**B**	took	**C**	made

24	**A**	shown	**B**	made	**C**	held

PART 5

QUESTIONS 25–30

For each question, write the correct answer.
Write **ONE** word for each gap.

Example: | **0** | *to* |

Welcome **(0)** .... my blog! My name is Mark and I'm 23 years old. I was born in

Australia, but I grew **(25)** .... in France. **(26)** .... the moment, I am working in

Paris, as a photographer for a fashion magazine.

I live near my office and **(27)** .... only takes me ten minutes to get there. Sometimes

I have to travel to other countries to work, **(28)** .... example, last month I went to

(29) .... USA to take photos at a big fashion show.

I get to meet a lot of very interesting people. Leave me a message **(30)** .... you want

to ask me any questions.

PART 6

QUESTION 31

You took part in a sports competition at the weekend.
Write an email to your English friend, Robbie.

In your email:

- say which sport the competition was for

- explain how you felt at the start of the competition

- say how well you did in the competition.

Write **25 words** or more.

Write the email on your answer sheet.

PART 7

QUESTION 32

Look at the three pictures.
Write the story shown in the pictures.
Write **35 words** or more.

Write the story on your answer sheet.

LISTENING (approximately 30 minutes)

PART 1

QUESTIONS 1–5

For each question, choose the correct answer.

---

1 How did the woman travel to work this morning?

A

B

C

2 What will the man eat first at the restaurant?

A

B

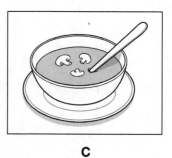

C

3 Which was the view from the woman's hotel room?

A

B

C

4 Why will the man miss the concert tonight?

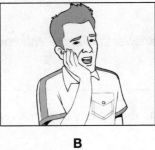
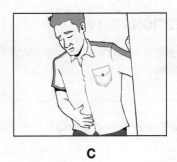

A	**B**	**C**

5 What will the woman wear for the party?

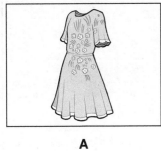

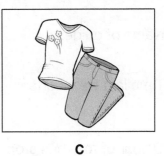

A	**B**	**C**

PART 2

QUESTIONS 6–10

For each question, write the correct answer in the gap. Write **one word** or a **number** or a **date** or a **time**.

You will hear a man giving information about a city bus tour.

City Bus Tours

Name of guide: Greg

Time last tour starts: (6) .... p.m.

Colour of tour bus stop: (7) ....

Length of tour: (8) .... minutes

Where to use ticket for discount: (9) ....

Place tour ends: (10) ....

PART 3

QUESTIONS 11–15

For each question, choose the correct answer.

___

You will hear two friends, Richard and Barbara, talking about a new supermarket.

11   What surprised Richard when he went to the supermarket?

    A   its size

    B   the time it opens

    C   the number of people there

12   This week, there are discounts on

    A   meat.

    B   fruit.

    C   vegetables.

13   What did Richard like most about the supermarket?

    A   the café

    B   the staff

    C   the music

14   What problem did Richard have at the supermarket?

    A   He didn't have any cash.

    B   He had to wait before he could pay.

    C   He couldn't use his credit card.

15   What does Barbara say about the car park?

    A   It's only for customers.

    B   It's quite far from the entrance.

    C   It's difficult to find.

PART 4

QUESTIONS 16–20

For each question, choose the correct answer.

---

16 You will hear a woman talking on the radio about her job.
What's her job?

A   engineer

B   mechanic

C   pilot

17 You will hear a woman talking to a friend about a film.
What does she say about the film?

A   It was funny.

B   It was true.

C   It was scary.

18 You will hear a sports coach talking to some footballers.
What would the coach like them to become better at?

A   running with the ball

B   getting goals

C   working as a team

19 You will hear two friends talking about a website.
Why does Julia prefer to buy clothes from the website?

A   It offers the latest fashions.

B   The discounts are excellent.

C   Orders always arrive quickly.

20 You will hear two colleagues talking together.
Why was the man not at the meeting this morning?

A   He had to go to the dentist.

B   He had other work to do.

C   He wasn't feeling well.

PART 5

QUESTIONS 21–25

For each question, choose the correct answer.

You will hear Gregory talking to Angelika about some things he has bought for his new house. What is he going to put in each place?

Example:

0	garden	H

Places

21	dining room	
22	bathroom	
23	bedroom	
24	living room	
25	kitchen	

Things

A	bookcase
B	clock
C	cupboard
D	curtains
E	lamp
F	mirror
G	seat
H	table

You now have 6 minutes to write your answers on the answer sheet.

Test 2

READING AND WRITING (60 minutes)

PART 1

QUESTIONS 1–6

For each question, choose the correct answer.

1

From: Cristina
To: Molly

Sorry, but I'm going to be late for our meeting about the new football team tomorrow. I'll probably arrive around 10.20 – start without me!

A Cristina says she might miss the meeting tomorrow.

B Cristina wants to change the time of tomorrow's meeting.

C Cristina is telling Molly not to wait for her tomorrow.

2

Sam's Café

Open daily: 6.00 a.m. – 3.00 p.m.

20% student discount:
6.00 a.m. – 10.00 a.m.

A The café is closed to students after 10 a.m.

B Students who come early get lower prices.

C Students cannot eat lunch here every day.

3

Tess.
Could I borrow your laptop tonight? Mine's at the computer repair shop. If not, do you know anyone who can lend me one?
Missie

A Missie is asking Tess to help her find a laptop to use.

B Missie is offering to lend her laptop to a friend.

C Missie wants to find someone to repair her laptop.

4

> ## SPECIAL OFFER UNTIL SATURDAY
>
> Shirts £10 each when you buy two!
>
> Usual price £25

A   This Saturday each shirt will cost £10 less than usual.

B   If you buy more than one shirt, you can save money.

C   After Saturday, the price of these shirts will go down.

5

Matt,
We're already at the cinema but can't see you anywhere. The film starts soon and Ben wants to get some snacks. Hurry up!
Dom

Why did Dom send this message?

A   He is worried they'll miss some of the film.

B   He wants to eat something before the film.

C   He needs to tell Matt where the cinema is.

6

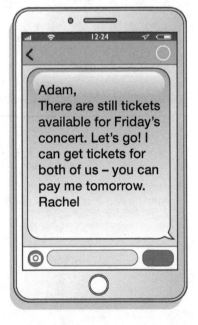

Adam,
There are still tickets available for Friday's concert. Let's go! I can get tickets for both of us – you can pay me tomorrow.
Rachel

Why did Rachel send this message?

A   to offer to buy a concert ticket for Adam

B   to find out more about the concert from Adam

C   to tell Adam what the concert tickets cost

PART 2

QUESTIONS 7–13

For each question, choose the correct answer.

		Petra	Bea	Sara
7	Who didn't enjoy tennis as much as other activities at the tennis centre?	A	B	C
8	Who had to change her plans for the future after an accident?	A	B	C
9	Who says she missed people from home while she was at the tennis centre?	A	B	C
10	Who went back to the tennis centre to learn to become a coach?	A	B	C
11	Who doesn't like the idea of travelling a lot for her job?	A	B	C
12	Who moved to a different country with a member of her family?	A	B	C
13	Who teaches tennis to young people who haven't played before?	A	B	C

How I became a tennis coach

Petra

I grew up in Germany, but when I was 17, I moved to Spain so I could go to a tennis centre there. It was hard to be without my family and friends, especially when I hurt myself or got ill. However, my tennis improved a lot. After three years, I left the centre and began my career. I started playing in big competitions around the world. I did OK, but wasn't earning enough money, so I quickly decided to become a tennis coach instead. I now teach children who are just starting the game, which is fun.

Bea

When I was 14, my dad sent me to a tennis centre near my home in Italy. He thought I might become a top player like him, but I saw how much time he spent going from one country to another during his career, and I've never wanted that for myself. My favourite things at the tennis centre were spending time at the pool or having barbecues with friends in the evenings. I'm now a coach, and teach young tennis stars at summer camps in Italy.

Sara

When I went to live in Spain so I could go to a famous tennis centre there, my dad came with me, and my mum stayed at home in Scotland. My tennis really improved during my two years there, but when I broke my foot it became clear that a career as a tennis player wasn't going to be possible. I went home for a year and then returned to the centre to do a coaching course. I now teach the best young players in Scotland.

PART 3

QUESTIONS 14–18

For each question, choose the correct answer.

Joining a ballroom dancing club

By Pippa Cartwright

When I started college, I wanted to find a club to join. One of the first ones I looked at was ballroom dancing – a type of dance you do with a partner. The people there seemed to be having a great time, and it didn't cost much, so I decided to join.

The first week I went, I was really worried because the teacher told us that there were nineteen different dances we had to learn. But it's been fine. When there's a new thing to learn, he shows it to us lots of times and makes sure we're all good at it before we do the next thing.

When I joined, I didn't know any of the other people in the club because we all study different subjects. But it's been a great way to meet people, and I've made some of my best friends in the club.

One of the reasons we learn the dances is to enter competitions. I couldn't wait to do my first one. Before we started, I was a bit worried. But during the competition, my partner and I remembered everything about our dances. We were great. We didn't win any prizes, but it didn't matter – we loved it!

Joining the ballroom dancing club has been fantastic. In the past, I always did the same sports and activities, year after year, but ballroom dancing has taught me there's nothing scary about doing something you've never tried before. I still do lots of sports, but now I can add ballroom dancing to my list of hobbies.

---

14   Why did Pippa join the dance club?

    A   She thought it looked fun.

    B   She didn't have to pay for it.

    C   She didn't like any of the other clubs.

15   What does Pippa say about the dance teacher?

    A   He teaches them a new dance every week.

    B   He often tells new members how good they are.

    C   He repeats new things until everyone can do them.

16   What does Pippa say about the other club members?

    A   She has become close to some of them.

    B   She is on the same course as some of them.

    C   She was friends with some of them before joining.

17   How did Pippa feel about her first dance competition?

    A   happy to win first prize

    B   upset that she forgot the dances

    C   excited to take part

18   In the final paragraph, Pippa says

    A   ballroom dancing is her favourite hobby.

    B   she's learned not to be afraid to do new things.

    C   she isn't sure which activity to try next.

PART 4

QUESTIONS 19–24

For each question, choose the correct answer.

Walter Bonatti

Walter Bonatti, one of the greatest alpine mountain climbers of all time, was born in Italy in 1930. As a child, he **(19)** .... his holidays in Bergamo with his uncles. He loved the mountains there, and at the age of 18, he **(20)** .... to climb the highest and most difficult ones. He was one of the **(21)** .... people to do this and he was very **(22)** .... at it.

He went on to climb many other mountains, including the famous K2 in the Himalayas. At the age of just 35, he decided to **(23)** .... his climbing career. However, he continued to work as a mountain guide and photographer. He also wrote several books about his climbing **(24)** ...., which are read in all Italian schools.

19	**A**	travelled	**B**	went	**C**	spent
20	**A**	became	**B**	began	**C**	turned
21	**A**	early	**B**	first	**C**	soon
22	**A**	successful	**B**	interested	**C**	popular
23	**A**	shut	**B**	close	**C**	end
24	**A**	experiences	**B**	occupations	**C**	subjects

PART 5

QUESTIONS 25–30

For each question, write the correct answer.
Write **ONE** word for each gap.

Example:

0	*at*

From: Bea

To: Tania

How are things? Are you busy **(0)** .... the moment? **(25)** .... you remember our conversation last weekend about going **(26)** .... the theatre? Well, the play 'Fathers and Sons' **(27)** .... showing next week at West Theatre. Shall **(28)** .... go and see it together? I've heard it's very good!

From: Tania

To: Bea

That sounds great! **(29)** .... would you like to go? I'm busy on Friday next week, **(30)** .... I'm free the other days. Shall I get the tickets? I can buy them online. We've both got student ID cards, so they won't be too expensive.

PART 6

QUESTION 31

Read the email from your English friend, Pat.

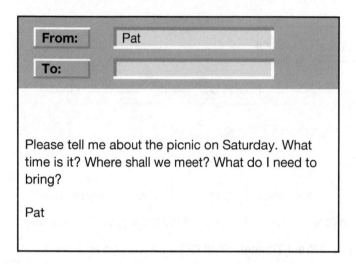

From: Pat

To:

Please tell me about the picnic on Saturday. What time is it? Where shall we meet? What do I need to bring?

Pat

Write an email to Pat and answer the questions.
Write **25 words** or more.

Write the email on your answer sheet.

PART 7

QUESTION 32

Look at the three pictures.
Write the story shown in the pictures.
Write **35 words** or more.

Write the story on your answer sheet.

LISTENING (approximately 30 minutes)

PART 1

QUESTIONS 1–5

For each question, choose the correct answer.

---

1   Where is the cup now?

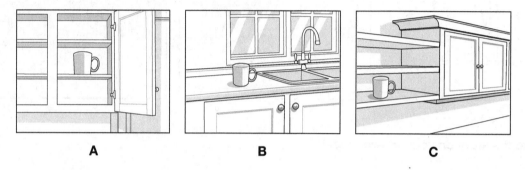

A   **B**   **C**

2   Who will Sally meet at the station?

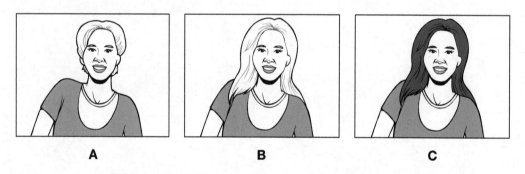

A   **B**   **C**

3   What did the man learn to do at the beach?

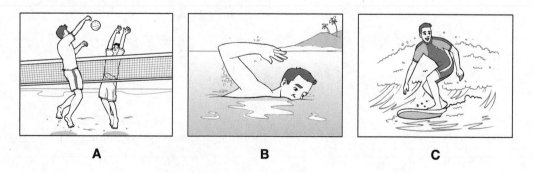

A   **B**   **C**

4 Where are they going to meet?

A   **B**   **C**

5 What didn't the man buy?

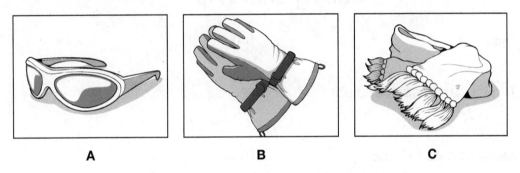

A   **B**   **C**

PART 2

QUESTIONS 6–10

For each question, write the correct answer in the gap. Write **one word** or a **number** or a **date** or a **time**.

You will hear a woman talking to sailing club members about a trip.

Sailing club trip

Date: 19th July

Time to arrive back at club: **(6)** .... p.m.

Name of café for lunch: **(7)** ....

Bring: **(8)** ....

Number of people: **(9)** ....

Secretary's name: **(10)** Ms ....

PART 3

QUESTIONS 11–15

For each question, choose the correct answer.

You will hear a manager, Victoria, talking to her assistant, Daniel, about the new company building.

11 How will staff find out about the new building?

    A   in an email

    B   at a meeting

    C   at a company meal

12 Why is the company moving to a new building?

    A   to save money

    B   to be in the town centre

    C   to have larger offices

13 When will staff start working in the new building?

    A   the end of May

    B   the beginning of July

    C   the middle of August

14 What does Daniel think the staff will enjoy most about the new area?

    A   the restaurants

    B   the shops

    C   the gym

15 What does Daniel need to order next?

    A   keys

    B   signs

    C   furniture

PART 4

QUESTIONS 16–20

For each question, choose the correct answer.

---

16   You will hear a woman, Jen, telling her friend about her favourite singer, Mikey.
      What's just happened?

    A   Jen's seen him on stage.

    B   Jen's taken a photo of him.

    C   Jen's had a conversation with him.

17   You will hear a man, Alex, talking to a friend about a tennis competition.
      Why didn't Alex do well in the competition?

    A   He was thirsty.

    B   He was hungry.

    C   He was tired.

18   You will hear two people talking at a tourist information centre.
      What advice does the man give the woman?

    A   Don't miss a special exhibition.

    B   Don't visit the museum today.

    C   Don't buy tickets too late.

19   You will hear two friends talking about what they did at the weekend.
      What didn't the woman do at the weekend?

    A   watch TV

    B   play sport

    C   go shopping

20   You will hear a man talking to his friend about his new flat.
      What's he going to do now?

    A   paint the flat

    B   turn the heating on

    C   move some furniture

PART 5

QUESTIONS 21–25

For each question, choose the correct answer.

___

You will hear a woman telling her brother about her friends and their hobbies.
What hobby does each friend have?

Example:

0	Simon	**B**

Friends

21	Jane	☐
22	Derek	☐
23	Mary	☐
24	Tony	☐
25	Sarah	☐

Hobbies

A	acting
B	art
C	cycling
D	making music
E	photography
F	reading
G	travelling
H	watching sport

You now have 6 minutes to write your answers on the answer sheet.

Test 3

READING AND WRITING (60 minutes)

PART 1
QUESTIONS 1–6

For each question, choose the correct answer.

1

> **Swimming pool closed
> for building work**
>
> **Open from Tuesday
> for lessons only**

A People who have swimming classes can go on Tuesday.

B The pool will be closed to all customers after Tuesday.

C Swimming lessons will be in a new pool on Tuesday.

2

> **Chess club members!**
>
> We're meeting in the library this Wednesday instead of the hall, as there's a dance show happening there at 7 p.m.

The chess club is

A on a different day this week.

B in a different place this week.

C at a different time this week.

3

> Rob,
> Leave your laptop in the kitchen before you go out and I'll see if I can find out why it's not working.
> Dad

Why did Rob's dad write this note?

A to ask if he can use Rob's laptop

B to tell Rob where he left his laptop

C to offer to check Rob's laptop

4

Mark,
I have to work until 6.00, so I can't meet you at the café. See you at the cinema instead, just before the film.
Rafa

A   Rafa needs to change the plans for this evening.

B   Rafa will eat at work before going to the cinema.

C   Rafa prefers to see the film at a later time.

5

Sightseeing trips twice daily

Buses – 9.00 a.m. & 2.00 p.m.

Tickets only available from tourist office

A   It's not possible to buy tickets on the bus.

B   Tourists must book both trips at 9.00 a.m.

C   Each sightseeing trip takes two hours.

6

Cinema park is full
Please use the free one in the shopping centre

A   You should pay for cinema parking in the shopping centre.

B   People who want to see a film must drive to the shopping centre cinema.

C   Cinema visitors should use a different car park.

PART 2

QUESTIONS 7–13

For each question, choose the correct answer.

		Paula	Sally	Kim
7	Who does her hobby with people in her family?	A	B	C
8	Who started classes after getting some good advice?	A	B	C
9	Who began her hobby after feeling unhappy at work?	A	B	C
10	Who did her hobby for a long time before starting classes?	A	B	C
11	Who has made new friends at her classes?	A	B	C
12	Who felt worried before starting her classes?	A	B	C
13	Who first had classes in her hobby as a child?	A	B	C

Learning for fun

Meet three women who enjoy taking classes in their free time.

Paula

I work full time as a nurse, and don't have much time for hobbies, but I've been interested in photography since I was a child. On my last holiday to India, I took lots of pictures, and everyone I showed them to said they were great. So I decided to do a course. At first, I was afraid I might not be good enough. After all, it was my first time as a student for ten years! But I loved it from the very first lesson.

Sally

When I was still at school, I started learning the violin. It was fun and I was quite good at it, but I didn't do it for long, because I had so many other hobbies. Then last year, I was having a hard time in my job, and my husband bought me a violin as a present. I started learning with a teacher again. All three of my children are learning to play instruments too, so now we can practise with each other!

Kim

Last year I moved to a new city because of my job. I didn't have anything to do in the evenings, so one of my colleagues said I should try a class at the local college. I immediately thought of cooking. My mum was a fantastic cook, and when I was a child I loved watching her in the kitchen, but I never learned how to cook myself. The other students on the course are around my age, and sometimes we go to restaurants together, or even the cinema.

PART 3

QUESTIONS 14–18

For each question, choose the correct answer.

My city

Pop singer Charlotte Bond talks about living in London.

I live in the centre of London. I love it because there's always something happening and there are people around whatever time it is. Famous people like it too – they often come here for the restaurants and shops.

I've lived here all my life. When I was little, I had singing lessons at a place near where I live now. I was afraid of the teacher at first, and some of the songs we did together were quite hard to learn. But she was good at what she did and I learned a lot of things that have helped me in my career.

When friends visit me now, I enjoy taking them sightseeing. You can get a bus around the city, but we prefer to walk. I've got a little car and I love driving, but there's so much traffic here, and it's hard to find parking spaces.

One building I love is the Natural History Museum. They sometimes hold parties there, and last December my band and I played at one. I'll never forget it. When I go to exhibitions at the museum with my friends, I tell them all about that night and how amazing it was.

Soon I'll be leaving London to go on tour with my band. We're playing in lots of new cities and I can't wait to explore them. We've sold lots of tickets, which is great. I'll be away from my family for six months, but they're coming to see me sing, so it's fine.

---

14   What does Charlotte love about the centre of London?

    A   It is always busy.

    B   Famous people often visit.

    C   The shops are very good.

15   How does Charlotte feel about the singing lessons she had?

    A   She's surprised she can remember them.

    B   She's sorry she didn't try harder.

    C   She's glad she did them.

16   What does Charlotte think is the best way to see the city?

    A   by car

    B   on foot

    C   by bus

17   Why does Charlotte love the Natural History Museum?

    A   She had a special experience there.

    B   She thinks the building is beautiful.

    C   She enjoys visiting the exhibitions.

18   What does Charlotte say about going on tour with her band?

    A   She hopes lots of people will buy tickets for her shows.

    B   She feels excited about seeing new places.

    C   She's worried she'll miss her family.

PART 4

QUESTIONS 19–24

For each question, choose the correct answer.

Camels

Camels are one of the only large animals that can live happily in the Sahara Desert. The hot weather and strong winds are not a **(19)** .... for them. Also, they do not need to eat or drink every day, and this **(20)** .... them very useful to the people who live there.

Camels begin working at the age of about four years old and don't stop until they are around 25 to 30. They can carry people or things a very long **(21)** ...., and because of this they are sometimes **(22)** .... the 'ships of the desert'.

These days, there are roads across some **(23)** .... of the Sahara, so buses and lorries are often **(24)** .... However, in places where there are no roads, camels are still the only type of transport.

19	**A**	trouble	**B**	mistake	**C**	problem
20	**A**	gets	**B**	has	**C**	makes
21	**A**	way	**B**	path	**C**	road
22	**A**	described	**B**	said	**C**	called
23	**A**	parts	**B**	examples	**C**	things
24	**A**	put	**B**	used	**C**	done

PART 5

QUESTIONS 25–30

For each question, write the correct answer.

Write **ONE** word for each gap.

Example:

0	*hope*

From:	Jenny
To:	David

Hi David,

I **(0)** .... you're well. It's my brother Tom's birthday **(25)** .... month, and I don't

know **(26)** .... to buy him for a present. Have you got **(27)** .... ideas? He's the

same age **(28)** .... you, and likes the same kind of things.

Thanks,

Jenny

From:	David
To:	Jenny

Hi Jenny,

I think I can help you! Why not get Tom a book? I've just read *Dragon Teeth*, which was

written **(29)** .... Michael Crichton. He's such a fantastic author! I loved it, and I think

(30) .... brother would like it too.

David

PART 6

QUESTION 31

Read the email from your English friend, Alex.

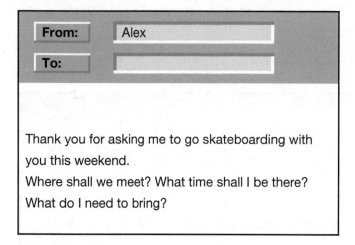

From: Alex

To:

Thank you for asking me to go skateboarding with you this weekend.

Where shall we meet? What time shall I be there?

What do I need to bring?

Write an email to Alex and answer the questions.
Write **25 words** or more.

Write the email on your answer sheet.

PART 7

QUESTION 32

Look at the three pictures.
Write the story shown in the pictures.
Write **35 words** or more.

Write the story on your answer sheet.

LISTENING (approximately 30 minutes)

PART 1

QUESTIONS 1–5

For each question, choose the correct answer.

---

1 Where will they go if it rains tomorrow?

A

B

C

2 Why didn't the woman buy the book?

A

B

C

3 Where does the man work now?

A

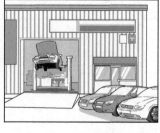

B

C

4 Where does the man want to go?

A   B   C

5 What's the man making?

A   B   C

PART 2

QUESTIONS 6–10

For each question, write the correct answer in the gap. Write **one word** or **a number** or **a date** or **a time**.

You will hear a man talking about a film on local radio.

New film

Name of film:	Runner
Subject of film:	(6) ....
Name of cinema:	(7) ....
Start date:	(8) ....
Start time:	(9) .... p.m.
Cost of student ticket:	(10) £..

PART 3

QUESTIONS 11–15

For each question, choose the correct answer.

You will hear Phil talking to his friend Jess about a new sports centre.

11 How did Jess find out about the new sports centre?

    A   She saw a poster.

    B   A friend of hers works there.

    C   She heard about it on the radio.

12 What doesn't Phil like about the sports centre?

    A   It's too noisy.

    B   It's very expensive.

    C   It's not big enough.

13 Phil prefers to go to the sports centre

    A   early in the morning.

    B   at the weekend.

    C   during working hours.

14 Why is the new swimming pool closed at the moment?

    A   They are cleaning it.

    B   There's a competition.

    C   The water's cold.

15 Members of the sports centre

    A   should buy special shoes.

    B   can get a discount in the café.

    C   needn't pay for exercise classes.

PART 4

QUESTIONS 16–20

For each question, choose the correct answer.

---

16   You will hear a woman talking to a friend about getting to work.
Why did the woman arrive at the office late?

A   The road was closed.

B   There was a problem with her car.

C   She couldn't find her car keys.

17   You will hear a man, Peter, talking to a friend about his plans.
Where will Peter be this Saturday?

A   at a party

B   in another country

C   on a boat

18   You will hear a man talking about a music festival.
What's different about the festival this year?

A   how long it is

B   where it is

C   when it is

19   You will hear two people talking about their school days.
Which subject did they both enjoy at school?

A   history

B   geography

C   science

20   You will hear someone speaking to customers in a supermarket.
What's cheaper in the supermarket this week?

A   desserts

B   soft drinks

C   fruit

PART 5

QUESTIONS 21–25

For each question, choose the correct answer.

_____

You will hear Helena talking to her friend Steve about hotels in their city.
What does Steve think about each hotel?

Example:

0	Plaza Hotel	**E**

_____

Hotels

			Opinions	
21	City Hotel	☐	**A**	comfortable beds
			B	expensive
22	The Bridge Hotel	☐		
			C	friendly staff
23	Lemontree Hotel	☐	**D**	good food
			E	hard to find
24	Greenleaf Hotel	☐	**F**	large bedrooms
			G	no parking
25	The International Hotel	☐		
			H	noisy

You now have 6 minutes to write your answers on the answer sheet.

Test 4

READING AND WRITING (60 minutes)

PART 1

QUESTIONS 1–6

For each question, choose the correct answer.

1

From: Jack
To: Football coach

I'm at the dentist's, so I won't be at football practice at 4 o'clock. I can get there for 4.30 – sorry.

A Jack doesn't want to go to football practice today.

B Jack won't be on time for today's football practice.

C Jack can't go to football practice today because he's at the dentist's.

2

Ollie,
I was late this morning, so I took your bike to go to college. I'll be back at 4 o'clock. I hope that's OK?
Leo

Leo wrote this message

A to ask Ollie what time they need to do something.

B to thank Ollie for doing something for him.

C to explain to Ollie why he has done something.

3

> ### Castle Restaurant
> These outside tables are for restaurant customers only
> Picnic tables by lake

A People must buy their food and drinks inside before they choose a table.

B People may sit here if they are eating food bought in this place.

C If you have brought your own sandwiches, you can eat them here.

4

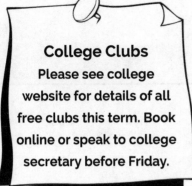

College Clubs
Please see college website for details of all free clubs this term. Book online or speak to college secretary before Friday.

A Students can check the cost of joining a club by going online.

B Students must decide what they want to do by the end of the week.

C Students must not book a club before speaking to the college secretary.

5

Weekend music festival

This entrance for people with tickets

Tickets for Sunday
available online

A If you don't have a ticket, you can't get in here.

B If you want a ticket for Sunday, you must wait here.

C If you go to another entrance, you can get a ticket.

6

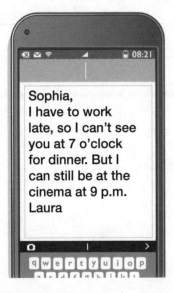

Sophia,
I have to work late, so I can't see you at 7 o'clock for dinner. But I can still be at the cinema at 9 p.m.
Laura

Why did Laura write this message?

A to invite Sophia to see a film with her

B to check when she needs to meet Sophia

C to let Sophia know about a change of plan

PART 2

QUESTIONS 7–13

For each question, choose the correct answer.

		Priya	Zoe	Heike
7	Who practises her dancing seven days a week?	A	B	C
8	Who feels scared before she goes on stage?	A	B	C
9	Who would like to try a different type of dance?	A	B	C
10	Who feels sad that she can't spend much time with her friends?	A	B	C
11	Who says she has no plans to change her job?	A	B	C
12	Who has a family member who is famous?	A	B	C
13	Who says the people she dances with are older than her?	A	B	C

A dancer's life

Priya

I work as a dancer, and I'm also studying part-time. I practise most days and have to do my college work, so I can't always go out with my friends at weekends, but that's fine. We text each other every day. I mostly dance in musicals, but in the future I'm hoping to start jazz dance. My mum always comes to watch me on stage. She's my biggest fan! Being a dancer isn't easy, but I want to do it as long as I can.

Zoe

There are dancers of all ages in my dance company and every year we go on international tours together. My cousin also dances with me. She's been a dancer for seven years and people everywhere know her now. She was a jazz dancer in the past, but loves what we do now. I don't usually feel worried before I dance in front of others – I know I'm good! But that's only because I try so hard. I spend about three hours dancing every day.

Heike

I come from a family of dancers so maybe it's not surprising I'm one too. I'm in a hip-hop group at the moment, but actually I can dance to any music – even jazz! I'm the youngest member of my dance group. Before each show, I think of everything that might go wrong, but I try hard to tell myself it'll all be OK. We dance all over the country, so I'm away from home almost every day and I miss my friends a lot.

PART 3

QUESTIONS 14–18

For each question, choose the correct answer.

Travel writer

Tim Greenwood lives in Oakland, USA. He has written about Cambodia, Thailand and India. At the moment he is writing a book about Nepal.

Tim, how did you start travelling?

We never travelled as a family, but when I was a teenager I saw movies like *Lawrence of Arabia* and they made me want to travel. I left college at the age of 21 and went to Europe alone. That trip didn't go well – I was too young and didn't know how to look after myself.

How did you start writing?

I've loved writing since I was ten – I've never wanted any other career. At 21, I wrote for my weekly college paper and then started writing travel articles. At first, none of the travel magazines I sent them to wanted to buy them, but that slowly changed. It took two or three years, I guess.

What do you find difficult about writing?

It is easy to spend all my time travelling and then not have time to open up my laptop and work! Also, it's hard to earn enough money. I'll never stop writing, but one day I may have to do a few hours a week teaching just to pay the bills.

What's the best thing about being a travel writer?

I get letters from young people who've read my books and articles and enjoy my work. I just love that!

---

14   As a teenager, Tim

    A   went on trips with his parents.

    B   became interested in seeing the world.

    C   spent too much time watching TV.

15   What does Tim say about his trip to Europe?

    A   He didn't have time to see everything.

    B   It was more fun than college.

    C   It was not a great success.

16   When Tim was 21, he couldn't

    A   travel as much as he wanted to.

    B   decide what to write about.

    C   sell many of his articles.

17   In the future, Tim thinks he might

    A   do some extra work.

    B   earn more from writing.

    C   change his job.

18   What does Tim like about being a travel writer?

    A   hearing from his fans

    B   giving advice to people

    C   meeting other young writers

PART 4

QUESTIONS 19–24

For each question, choose the correct answer.

An unusual holiday

Most people go on holiday to get away from work. But in the beautiful Scottish village of Wigtown, it's **(19)** .... to rent a flat above a bookshop, and work as the **(20)** .... of the bookshop for a week. This holiday is very popular with people who love books and who have always **(21)** .... their own bookshop.

However, this is a holiday, so people staying there don't have to work very hard. They can **(22)** .... the opening hours of the shop, and they just have a few jobs to do, such as **(23)** .... the shelves with books.

Guests also get a bike, so they can **(24)** .... the area when the shop is closed. The holiday is so popular that the flat is fully booked for the next three years.

19	**A** able	**B** possible	**C** available
20	**A** manager	**B** colleague	**C** customer
21	**A** hoped	**B** wanted	**C** decided
22	**A** think	**B** find	**C** choose
23	**A** putting	**B** adding	**C** filling
24	**A** look	**B** ride	**C** explore

PART 5

QUESTIONS 25–30

For each question, write the correct answer.

Write **ONE** word for each gap.

Example:

0	*with*

From: Cara

To: Ashley

I'm in Ireland staying **(0)** .... my friend and we're having a great holiday. My friend's

house is near the sea, so we can **(25)** .... swimming every day, and there are

lots of other things to do as well. Yesterday we rode horses on the beach and had

(26) .... lovely picnic in the mountains.

How are you? **(27)** .... you been on holiday yet? I'll be back home at the weekend.

(28) .... you want to go to the cinema **(29)** .... week? There's a new film I really

want to see. Please **(30)** .... me know.

PART 6

QUESTION 31

You want to go to the shopping centre on Saturday with your English friend, Alex.
Write an email to Alex.

In your email:

- ask Alex to go to the shopping centre with you on Saturday
- say what you need to buy
- explain how you will travel there.

Write **25 words** or more.

Write the email on your answer sheet.

PART 7

QUESTION 32

Look at the three pictures.
Write the story shown in the pictures.
Write **35 words** or more.

Write the story on your answer sheet.

LISTENING (approximately 30 minutes)

PART 1

QUESTIONS 1–5

For each question, choose the correct answer.

---

1   What was the weather like for the football match?

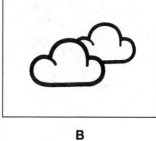
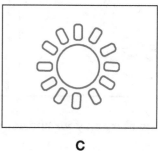

A   **B**   **C**

2   What sport is the woman going to start doing soon?

A   **B**   **C**

3   Why was the man late for work?

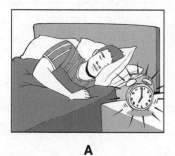

A   **B**   **C**

4 Which food is the man eating?

A   B   C

5 What has the man had problems with?

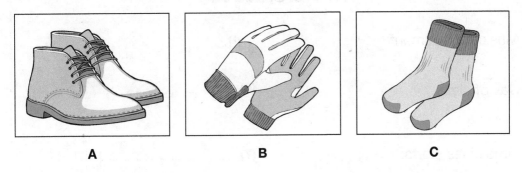

A   B   C

PART 2

QUESTIONS 6–10

For each question, write the correct answer in the gap. Write **one word** or a **number** or a **date** or a **time**.

You will hear some information about music classes at a local college.

Music classes

Musical instrument: guitar

Day of class: **(6)** ....

Time class starts: **(7)** .... p.m.

Room for beginners' class: **(8)** ....

Teacher's name: **(9)** Mrs ....

Month of rock concert: **(10)** ....

PART 3

QUESTIONS 11–15

For each question, choose the correct answer.

You will hear a man, Ben, and a woman, Emma, talking about Ben's new flat.

11 When did Ben go to live in his new flat?

    A   two days ago

    B   two weeks ago

    C   two months ago

12 How is Ben's new flat different from his old one?

    A   It is nearer to his job.

    B   It has better views.

    C   It is larger.

13 Which room in the new flat does Ben like best?

    A   the bathroom

    B   the living room

    C   the bedroom

14 What has Emma given Ben for his new flat?

    A   shelves

    B   carpets

    C   curtains

15 Who lives in the flat next to Ben's?

    A   a mechanic

    B   a journalist

    C   a police officer

PART 4

QUESTIONS 16–20

For each question, choose the correct answer.

---

16 You will hear a man asking for help with his computer.
What's the problem with it?

    A   The computer won't turn off.

    B   The keyboard isn't working.

    C   The screen isn't bright enough.

17 You will hear a woman talking to her husband.
Where are they planning to meet the woman's brother?

    A   at the railway station

    B   at the airport

    C   at their home

18 You will hear an explorer talking on the radio.
What was the last place that he visited?

    A   a mountain

    B   a desert

    C   an island

19 You will hear a man talking to his sister about his new phone.
Why did he choose this phone?

    A   because it's really light

    B   because it looks modern

    C   because it has a good camera

20 You will hear two colleagues talking about a meeting.
How do they feel after the meeting?

    A   pleased

    B   worried

    C   tired

PART 5

QUESTIONS 21–25

For each question, choose the correct answer.

You will hear Larry talking to Cara about a friend's birthday.
What present will each person give?

Example:

0	Cara	**A**

People

Presents

21	Anthea	

| 22 | Larry | |

| 23 | Kerry | |

| 24 | Tony | |

| 25 | Hannah | |

A	art equipment
B	bag
C	book
D	chocolate
E	concert ticket
F	jewellery
G	perfume
H	picture

You now have 6 minutes to write your answers on the answer sheet.

Sample answer sheet: Reading and Writing

Draft

OFFICE USE ONLY - DO NOT WRITE OR MAKE ANY MARK ABOVE THIS LINE   Page 1 of 1

Cambridge Assessment
English

Candidate Name		Candidate Number	
Centre Name		Centre Number	
Examination Title		Examination Details	
Candidate Signature		Assessment Date	

Supervisor: If the candidate is ABSENT or has WITHDRAWN shade here ○

Key Reading and Writing Candidate Answer Sheet

Instructions
Use a PENCIL (B or HB).
Rub out any answer you want to change with an eraser.

For Parts 1, 2, 3 and 4:
Mark ONE letter for each answer.
For example: If you think A is the right answer to the question, mark your answer sheet like this:

0 [A] B C

For Part 5:
Write your answers clearly in the spaces next to the numbers (25 to 30) like this:

0 | E N G L I S H

Write your answers in CAPITAL LETTERS.

Part 1		Part 2		Part 3		Part 4	
1	A B C	7	A B C	14	A B C	19	A B C
2	A B C	8	A B C	15	A B C	20	A B C
3	A B C	9	A B C	16	A B C	21	A B C
4	A B C	10	A B C	17	A B C	22	A B C
5	A B C	11	A B C	18	A B C	23	A B C
6	A B C	12	A B C			24	A B C
		13	A B C				

Part 5

		Do not write below here			Do not write below here
25		25 1 0 ○ ○	28		28 1 0 ○ ○
26		26 1 0 ○ ○	29		29 1 0 ○ ○
27		27 1 0 ○ ○	30		30 1 0 ○ ○

Put your answers to Writing Parts 6 and 7 on the separate Answer Sheet

OFFICE USE ONLY - DO NOT WRITE OR MAKE ANY MARK BELOW THIS LINE   Page 1 of 1

Draft

© UCLES 2019   Photocopiable

Draft

OFFICE USE ONLY - DO NOT WRITE OR MAKE ANY MARK ABOVE THIS LINE

Cambridge Assessment
English

Candidate Name

Candidate Number

Centre Name

Centre Number

Examination Title

Examination Details

Candidate Signature

Assessment Date

Supervisor: If the candidate is ABSENT or has WITHDRAWN shade here ○

Key Writing

Candidate Answer Sheet for Parts 6 and 7

INSTRUCTIONS TO CANDIDATES

Make sure that your name and candidate number are on this sheet.

Write your answers to Writing Parts 6 and 7 on the other side of this sheet.

Use a pencil.

You **must** write within the grey lines.

Do **not** write on the bar codes.

OFFICE USE ONLY - DO NOT WRITE OR MAKE ANY MARK BELOW THIS LINE

Draft

© UCLES 2019   Photocopiable

Sample answer sheet: Reading and Writing

Draft

Part 6: Write your answer below.

Part 7: Write your answer below.

Examiner's Use Only

Part 6	C	O	L

Part 7	C	O	L

Draft

© UCLES 2019   Photocopiable

Draft

OFFICE USE ONLY - DO NOT WRITE OR MAKE ANY MARK ABOVE THIS LINE   Page 1 of 1

Cambridge Assessment
English

Candidate Name		Candidate Number	
Centre Name		Centre Number	
Examination Title		Examination Details	
Candidate Signature		Assessment Date	

Supervisor: If the candidate is ABSENT or has WITHDRAWN shade here ○

Key Listening Candidate Answer Sheet

Instructions

Use a PENCIL (B or HB).
Rub out any answer you want to change with an eraser.

For Parts 1, 3, 4 and 5:
Mark ONE letter for each answer.
For example: If you think A is the right answer to the question, mark your answer sheet like this:

For Part 2:
Write your answers clearly in the spaces next to the numbers (6 to 10) like this:

0 E N G L I S H

Write your answers in CAPITAL LETTERS.

Part 1

	A	B	C
1	○	○	○
2	○	○	○
3	○	○	○
4	○	○	○
5	○	○	○

Part 2

		Do not write below here
6		6 1 ○ 0 ○
7		7 1 ○ 0 ○
8		8 1 ○ 0 ○
9		9 1 ○ 0 ○
10		10 1 ○ 0 ○

Part 3

	A	B	C
11	○	○	○
12	○	○	○
13	○	○	○
14	○	○	○
15	○	○	○

Part 4

	A	B	C
16	○	○	○
17	○	○	○
18	○	○	○
19	○	○	○
20	○	○	○

Part 5

	A	B	C	D	E	F	G	H
21	○	○	○	○	○	○	○	○
22	○	○	○	○	○	○	○	○
23	○	○	○	○	○	○	○	○
24	○	○	○	○	○	○	○	○
25	○	○	○	○	○	○	○	○

OFFICE USE ONLY - DO NOT WRITE OR MAKE ANY MARK BELOW THIS LINE   Page 1 of 1

Draft

© UCLES 2019   Photocopiable

Acknowledgements

The authors and publishers acknowledge the following sources of copyright material and are grateful for the permissions granted. While every effort has been made, it has not always been possible to identify the sources of all the material used, or to trace all copyright holders. If any omissions are brought to our notice, we will be happy to include the appropriate acknowledgements on reprinting and in the next update to the digital edition, as applicable.

Photographs

Key: T = Test, RW = Reading & Writing, P = Part.

All the photographs are sourced from Getty Images.

T2 RW P2: XiFotos/iStock/Getty Images Plus; Dougal Waters/DigitalVision; SolStock/E+;
T3 RW P2: Javier Sánchez Mingorance/EyeEm; Terry Vine/Blend Images; Bradley Olson/EyeEm;
T4 RW P2: Jose Luis Pelaez Inc/DigitalVision; MaFelipe/E+; Hero Images.

Typeset by QBS Learning.

Audio production by Real Deal Productions and dsound recording Ltd.

Visual materials for the Speaking test

Test 1
Do you like these different types of food?

Test 2

Do you like these different ways of travelling?

Test 3

Do you like these different free-time activities?

Test 4

Do you like these different sports?